A guide to discovery of the Castle, its Builders, and Neighbors.

Courtesy Sharlot Hall Museum, Prescott

(2)

April, 1894

"We rode along and finally Montezuma Castle loomed up... I was very much excited and filled with awe! We just sat and gazed. Finally I got my little wooden camera out and took a picture of the Castle from horseback."

F. Y. Steenberg

The Settlers

Many early visitors thought this cliff dwelling was a "castle" built by Aztec refugees for their emperor, Montezuma — thus the name!

Today

Thanks to the archeologist, a more realistic story is beginning to unfold. The setting is a prehistoric one, meaning the people involved left no written history. They are believed to be the ancestors of some present-day Southwestern Indians.

Montezuma Castle

Time A.D. 1100 - 1400

This 20-room apartment house was occupied between 1100 and 1400. It has approximately the same floor space as a large, three-bedroom home of today. Perhaps a dozen families, or about 50 people, lived here.

A natural recess provides shelter

Like other nearby caves and crevasses, the large recess in which the Castle was built is the product of wind and water erosion over eons of time. Shelter from the elements and solar heat from the winter sun were probably good reasons for starting a home here. Other ideas have also been suggested, including protection, tradition, or perhaps the view! However, with no written records to guide us, maybe the real reasons will never be known.

300 years of construction

The uppermost wall of the Castle was apparently the first one constructed. It makes two rooms out of a cave in the highest part of the recess. Later additions were made in front of and below these rooms. It appears that modifications were made right up to the time of abandonment!

Inside the Castle

A ROOF BEAM chopped to length with a stone axe. Was the notch at the end used to help lift the log in place?

INSIDE A TYPICAL ROOM. Uprights and ceiling beams are from sycamore trees. Ceilings and upper-story floors are a thatching of grasses and shrubs covered with a mud mortar. The small, T-shaped doorway may have helped in regulating air circulation.

WALLS OF ROCK CEMENTED TOGETHER WITH MUD. Note the handprints of the original plasterer.

Today

Because of the natural overhang and quality of construction, Montezuma Castle stands today as a well-preserved cliff dwelling.

Say Ranger!

The following are some frequently asked questions about Montezuma Castle

HOW DID THEY GET UP THERE? Probably ladders. Although none were found here, remains of ladders have been found at other prehistoric sites. Are there any materials around here from which they could make ladders? Sycamore and Ash are abundant along the fertile riverbed of nearby Beaver Creek.

THESE PEOPLE HAD NO WRITTEN HISTORY. HOW THEN DO WE KNOW ABOUT THEIR LIVES AND TIMES? The large mound at the base of the cliff contains over three centuries of trash discarded by the cliff dwellers above. As the layers of food-remains, wornout tools and broken pottery accumulated, an unwritten history of the lives and times of these people was provided. What will our dumps and landfills "tell" future archeologists about our lifestyles?

WHY CAN'T WE GO UP THERE?
Montezuma Castle is irreplaceable!
Most of the structure is over 600
years old and once housed about
50 people. Nearly one-half million
people now view this ruin yearly. If
the Castle had been open to
visitors last year, what would be
left for you to enjoy?

**ARE THESE OPENINGS AN
ENTRANCE TO THE CASTLE?**
No! These two small caves were
probably used for food storage.
Being high and dry, such walled-up
openings were excellent places to
store staples.

Not So Obvious

High and Dry

Slightly lower and to the west of the castle, there once stood an 8- or 9-room dwelling. Over the centuries natural weathering has reduced this structure to a pile of rocks and dust. Perhaps the people who built in the cliffs chose this site because they understood desert creeks. Occasionally, the flats below are covered by floodwaters.

For the future

This ruin has never been excavated. Wouldn't doing so add to our knowledge of its occupants? Probably. But instead of calling in the archeologists today, why not leave this site undisturbed for a while longer? Archeology is a relatively new science and its techniques are continually being developed and refined. Could the information buried here be of greater value in the future?

(9)

A Day In Their Life

Castle 'A'

West of Montezuma Castle, at the base of the cliff, is Castle A. In 1934 the ruin was excavated by archeologists. This "dig" provided insight into the lives of the families who called it home. Let's step back in time and join the archeologists in a few of these discoveries. . . .

Abandoned belongings

In one room, scattered here and there were corncobs, squash stems, beans, and the remains of several stone hoes. A large clay storage pot was found in the right rear corner. By its side, a food grinder was propped up and ready for use. Did we discover the remains of a farmer's home?

Tragedy

Buried in the room directly behind and above the preceding one were the remains of three infants. The Hopi Indians of northern Arizona believe in burying a child near the mother so that its spirit may enter another newborn. Does the discovery of these burials shed light on the spiritual beliefs of the parents?

Clever housekeeping

In a room to the left of the child burials a large clay pot was found propped against a firepit. Was this arrangement accidental? Or, did some prehistoric housekeeper devise a method for keeping water hot?

A touch of elegance

The caves above contained woven material. Many were made from wild plant fibers for day-to-day use —sandals, skirts, matting, and rope. Other items were woven from cotton, a cultivated "crop." Some of these fabrics were of dyed yarn and made into intricate designs. Today, weaving is considered an art. Would these prehistoric people agree?

. . . And Death

The Burials Reveal

Trading

Material goods are frequently found with human remains. Examine the pictures on these pages. These items were discovered with one of the female burials. The pendant and decorated bowl indicate that these people were part of an extensive trading network which covered at least the length and breadth of the Southwest.

Rigors of life

Of the fifteen skeletons whose ages could be determined, eleven died before age 45. Some skeletons also provided evidence of arthritis and other bone diseases. And as noted in the archeological report, ". . . two male skulls showed. . . several straight, ragged cuts such as could have been caused by a blunt stone axe."

The DECORATED BOWL was made in northeastern Arizona about 1350-1400.

The PLAIN BOWL was probably made locally.

Shell for the background of this NECKLACE PENDANT is from the southern California coast. The turquoise is probably from an area rich in copper.

Customs

The backs of over half the skulls were flattened! This could have occurred because infants were often strapped to rigid cradleboards. Whether this deformation was intentional or not is debatable.

Ponder for a moment

If archeologists examine our gravesites 600 years from now, what will they learn about us?

Survival

Beaver Creek flows regardless of the season! Most of the time it is gentle and clear. However, dry periods may reduce streamflow to a trickle hidden beneath the rocky creekbed. Limbs and twigs are often lodged in the trees along the creek. This debris is evidence of the power and height of rampaging flood waters. The cliff dwellers probably knew and accepted all these moods.

Directly across the creek, buried beneath years of river deposits, are remnants of prehistoric irrigation ditches. They were used to carry creek water into cultivated fields of corn, beans, squash and cotton.

These farmers also gathered the wild plants and hunted the animals along this streamside.

Keep an eye out for animals! Bones of deer, rabbit, squirrel, snake, turtle, fish and bird were found in the cliff dwellers' trash mounds.

— *Babs Monroe*

Today, this tree-lined creek provides a relaxing change from the more arid surroundings. To the prehistoric cliff dweller it meant survival.

A
Neighborhood

Archeologists suggest that this was a community of friends, relatives, and neighbors. People going about their daily chores — talking about the weather and the new family next door — or inquiring into the recent death of a newborn or elderly relative.

This village grew and flourished for over 300 years. And yet, when the pilgrims stepped onto Plymouth Rock in 1620, this prehistoric community had been abandoned for over 200 years.

Montezuma Castle National Monument preserves only a few of the hundreds of similar prehistoric ruins discovered in this area.

A *again the same sad story*
applies to the ruins. . .
all were forsaken, deserted.

*Over the centuries they have stood
there, empty, forlorn, but ever lovely in
the perfection of the dream which created
them.*

From the CLIFF DWELLERS
by W.E.S. Folsom-Dickerson

(19)

MONTEZUMA WELL

The "Well," as it is commonly called, is a separate unit of this National Monument. It is an area rich in cultural and natural history.

Geologists suggest that the Well is a sinkhole formed by water percolating through limestone. Warm, underground springs supply a daily flow of 1½ million gallons, and support a pond life devoid of fish! Nearby are the fossilized remains of irrigation ditches used to carry this water to prehistoric farmlands. Along the Well's rim are the ruins of these farmers' homes. Today, the water from Montezuma Well irrigates a nicely shaded picnic area abundant in bird life.